63

Hamlyn all-colour cookbooks

Meals in a Hurry

Marguerite Patten

Hamlyn
London · New York · Sydney · Toronto

Published by
The Hamlyn Publishing Group Limited
London · New York · Sydney · Toronto
Hamlyn House, Feltham, Middlesex, England

ISBN 0 600 30197 4
Printed in England by Sir Joseph Causton and Sons Limited
Line drawings by John Scott Martin

Contents

Useful facts and figures

Note on metrication

In this book quantities are given in both Imperial and metric measures. Exact conversion from Imperial to metric does not always give very convenient working quantities so for greater convenience and ease of working we have taken an equivalent of 25 grammes/millilitres to the ounce/fluid ounce. 1 oz. is exactly 28·35 g. and ¼ pint (5 fl. oz.) is 142 ml., so you will see that by using the unit of 25 you will get a slightly smaller result than the Imperial measures would give.

Occasionally, for example in a basic recipe such as a Victoria sandwich made with 4 oz. flour, butter and sugar and 2 eggs, we have rounded the conversion up to give a more generous result. For larger amounts where the exact conversion is not critical, for instance in soups or stews, we have used kilogrammes and fractions (1 kg. equals 2·2 lb.) and litres and fractions (1 litre equals 1·76 pints). All recipes have been individually converted so that each recipe preserves the correct proportions.

Oven temperatures

The following chart gives the Celsius (Centigrade) equivalents recommended by the Electricity Council.

Description	Fahrenheit	Celsius	Gas Mark
Very cool	225	110	¼
	250	130	½
Cool	275	140	1
	300	150	2
Moderate	325	170	3
	350	180	4
Moderately hot	375	190	5
	400	200	6
Hot	425	220	7
	450	230	8
Very hot	475	240	9

Introduction

Many housewives today run a home and also have a full- or part-time job. Others are kept fully occupied with home and children, but everyone finds the same thing – that even with all the labour-saving equipment we can now have in our houses, the days are still too short to fit in everything we have to do. Providing satisfying and nourishing meals for our family and friends can be one of the most time-consuming of our tasks.

This book contains recipes for the many people today who like good food and who must provide well-balanced and tasty meals for their families and guests without spending too much time on cooking. All the recipes are quick to prepare and enable you to put together a good meal with the minimum of effort. I have included recipes for starters, main dishes and sweets. You will notice that there are several recipes using fish; this is because fish is an excellent food, full of protein and rich in vitamins, and yet is very quick and easy to prepare in various delicious ways. Every recipe has a photograph opposite, particularly helpful when you are in a hurry as you can see at a glance what the recipe should look like, and the pictures will give you ideas for making up menus. At the top of every recipe I have given cooking times and approximate preparation times to help you plan your cooking.

I hope you will enjoy using this book and that it will help you to provide for your family the nourishing meals that they need, however busy your life.

Fruit as an hors d'oeuvre

Many fruits or fruit juices make an interesting start to a meal.

Citrus fruits

1. Serve fresh or canned orange juice as cold as possible. To give a new flavour, pour the juice over mint leaves, bruised to bring out the maximum flavour. Strain into frosted glasses and top with glacé or Maraschino cherries. To frost glasses brush the citrus with a little egg white and roll in castor sugar.
2. Mix orange, lemon and pineapple juice together.
3. Serve fresh grapefruit mixed with segments of fresh orange and tangerine, and moistened with lemon juice to give a 'bite'.
4. Mix segments of grapefruit with shellfish, toss in oil, vinegar or lemon juice, season well or blend with yoghurt and lemon juice.
5. Roll thin slices of ham round chopped skinned segments of grapefruit, orange and grated raw apple; blend with mayonnaise.

Melon

Cut the melon into slices, remove the seeds, then cut the flesh into neat portions. Top with thin slices of orange and glacé or Maraschino cherries. Serve with powdered ginger and sugar.

Glazed melon

Cut the melon into slices, sprinkle very lightly with powdered ginger and brown sugar then put under the grill for 2 minutes until the sugar melts. Serve at once. Serve slices of melon with Parma ham.

Pear

Ripe pears, peeled, cored and sliced, can also be served with Parma ham. Sprinkle the segments of pear with lemon juice to prevent them from turning brown.

Fig

Ripe dessert figs or well drained canned figs are another good accompaniment to Parma ham (this is the uncooked smoked ham).

Tomato

Flavour canned or bottled tomato juice with a little celery salt, sherry and Worcestershire sauce.

Avocado pears as an hors d'oeuvre

These imported fruits are becoming extremely popular in this country. Although they are called pears, the flavour bears no resemblance to ordinary pears, it is a smooth, rich creamy taste.

Avocado pears vinaigrette
Halve the pears, remove the stone in each, then fill the centre of each halved pear with French dressing. If wished this dressing, also known as vinaigrette, can be given a sharper taste with extra vinegar or lemon juice.

Avocado pears with shellfish
Prepare the pears by halving them, then taking out the stones. Fill with shrimps, prawns, or flaked crab meat or lobster blended either with mayonnaise with a little extra lemon juice added, or with the dressing used for Prawn cocktail, (see page 13). If preferred use just the French dressing with the fish.

Avocado pears with grapefruit
Pull the skin away from the flesh of the pear, then cut this into neat slices, discarding the stone. Sprinkle with lemon juice or with French dressing. Arrange on a bed of crisp lettuce with segments of fresh or well drained canned grapefruit. Top with mayonnaise.

Avocado pears indienne
Blend a little curry powder with mayonnaise, toss the shellfish in this before putting into the centre of the pears. Serve with wedges of lemon.

Avocado pears and cheese
Crumble Danish blue cheese and blend with mayonnaise; fill the centres of the pears with this mixture.

Baked avocado pears
Halve the pears, remove the pulp carefully, and blend with seasoning, a little lemon juice and oil. Pile back into the skins, top with crumbs and a little grated cheese and bake for 15 minutes in a hot oven (425–450°F., 220–230°C., Gas Mark 7–8).

Note: Avocado pears will discolour when cut unless sprinkled with lemon juice.

Prawn cocktail

Preparation time: 15 minutes plus time to make mayonnaise
Main utensils: sharp knife, basin
Serves: 4

Imperial
4 oz. prawns (weight when skinned, see stage 1)
lettuce
Dressing:
4 tablespoons mayonnaise (see page 89)
½–1 tablespoon tomato purée or ketchup
1 teaspoon Worcestershire sauce (see note)
2 tablespoons thick cream
seasoning

Metric
100 g. prawns (weight when skinned, see stage 1)
lettuce
Dressing:
4 tablespoons mayonnaise (see page 89)
½–1 tablespoon tomato purée or ketchup
1 teaspoon Worcestershire sauce (see note)
2 tablespoons thick cream
seasoning

1. If using frozen prawns, defrost at room temperature. To hasten the process the packet could be put into cold water for a while; do not put in hot water otherwise the fish will be tough.

If using fresh prawns, put them for 1 minute in hot water and the skins (or shells as they are often called) come away quickly and easily. Leave a few whole for garnish.

2. Blend all the ingredients together for the dressing.

3. Toss the prawns in the dressing.

4. Shred the lettuce very finely, for it has to be eaten with a spoon.

5. Put the lettuce into the glasses, top with the prawns and garnish with the reserved whole prawns as in the photograph. Serve with brown bread and butter and lemon.

Note: This can be increased up to 1 tablespoon if you want a more piquant flavour; or use a few drops of chilli sauce or soy sauce.

Variation

Use any other shellfish. To be economical use a mixture of cooked flaked white fish and shellfish.

Cheese and grapefruit salad

Preparation time: 10 minutes plus time to stand
Main utensil: sharp knife
Serves: 4

Imperial	**Metric**
2 grapefruit	2 grapefruit
6 oz. Cheddar cheese	150 g. Cheddar cheese
½ small red or green pepper	½ small red or green pepper
juice of grapefruit	juice of grapefruit
1 tablespoon olive oil	1 tablespoon olive oil
sugar (optional)	sugar (optional)
seasoning	seasoning
To garnish:	*To garnish:*
lettuce	lettuce

1. Halve the grapefruit on a plate.
2. Remove the segments carefully, put them in a basin, and discard any pips; cut away the skin.
3. Dice the Cheddar cheese and chop the red pepper, discarding the core and seeds; mix with the grapefruit.
4. Pour the juice from the grapefruit into a separate basin and blend with the olive oil, sugar and seasoning.
5. Pour the dressing over the cheese mixture and leave for about 30 minutes for the dressing to flavour the other ingredients.
6. Line the halved grapefruit cases with lettuce and pile the salad in the centre.

Serve as a light main dish with crisp toast or brown bread and butter.

Variations

Use orange segments and serve in sundae glasses. Top halved peaches with grated cheese or fill centres of pineapple rings with cheese blended with mayonnaise.

Ham and apple salad

Preparation time: 10 minutes
Main utensil: sharp knife
Serves: 4

Imperial
3 dessert apples
juice of 1 lemon
small head celery
bunch radishes
12 oz. cooked ham
French or vinaigrette dressing:
1 teaspoon made mustard
pinch salt
shake pepper
pinch sugar
1–1½ tablespoons vinegar
or lemon juice
2–3 tablespoons oil
1 tablespoon parsley

Metric
3 dessert apples
juice of 1 lemon
small head celery
bunch radishes
300 g. cooked ham
French or vinaigrette dressing:
1 teaspoon made mustard
pinch salt
shake pepper
pinch sugar
1–1½ tablespoons vinegar
or lemon juice
2–3 tablespoons oil
1 tablespoon parsley

1. Wipe but do not peel the apples. Core them, and cut into neat fingers; sprinkle with lemon juice.
2. Chop the celery; slice most of the radishes, leaving a few whole.
3. Cut the ham into neat fingers.
4. To make the dressing, blend the mustard with the other seasonings and the sugar. Mix in the vinegar, then work in the oil and beat thoroughly.
5. Add chopped parsley to the dressing.
6. Toss all ingredients in the dressing. Serve as cold as possible.

Variations
This salad can be made using cold cooked brisket of beef, lamb, veal or tongue; corned beef, luncheon meat and salami are also good.

Salami salad

Preparation time: 10 minutes plus time for radish waterlilies
Main utensils: sharp knife, cocktail sticks
Serves: 4

Imperial	Metric
French or vinaigrette dressing (see preceding recipe)	French or vinaigrette dressing (see preceding recipe)
8–12 oz. salami	200–300 g. salami
1–2 hard-boiled eggs	1–2 hard-boiled eggs
2 dessert apples	2 dessert apples
beetroot	beetroot
radishes	radishes
lettuce	lettuce

1. Make the French dressing as directed in the preceding recipe.
2. Slice salami thinly, keep covered until ready to use. Slice hard-boiled eggs. Peel the apple and cut into fingers, dip in dressing to prevent it turning brown.
3. Roll slices of salami round the apple, secure with cocktail sticks.
4. Cut beetroot into slices.
5. Cut the radishes in a vandyke pattern with a sharp knife. Put into cold water and leave for $\frac{3}{4}$–1 hour until they open out like waterlilies.
6. Put the washed lettuce in a serving bowl and arrange the beetroot, radishes, egg and salami and apple rolls on top. Serve with mayonnaise (see page 89) or additional French dressing.

Cottage cheese and corn salad

Preparation time: few minutes
Main utensil: large bowl
Serves: 4

Imperial	**Metric**
12 oz. cottage cheese	300 g. cottage cheese
French dressing (see page 17)	French dressing (see page 17)
1 can corn or corn and pepper	1 can corn or corn and pepper
few tomatoes	few tomatoes
cucumber	cucumber
chicory	chicory
spring onions	spring onions
radishes	radishes

1. Arrange the cottage cheese in the centre of a dish.
2. Make the dressing as directed.
3. Drain the corn and toss in French dressing. Arrange round the cottage cheese.
4. Garnish with quarters of tomato, sliced cucumber tossed in French dressing, quartered chicory, spring onions and radishes. Serve as cold as possible.

Variations

Many other cheeses are suitable for a salad. These are the most usual:

Cheddar: Close, creamy texture. Flavour deepens as cheese matures.

Cheshire: Mellow, open textured. Choose red or white.

Lancashire: Mild flavour when young, more pungent flavour as it matures. Loose texture. Try Sage Lancashire.

Demi-sel: Soft pasteurised cheese with a good 'bite'.

Cream cheese: Soft and mild.

Camembert: Best when ripe, i.e., soft and yielding.

Chicken salad with savoury cottage cheese sauce

Cooking time: few minutes
Preparation time: 10 minutes
Main cooking utensil: saucepan
Serves: 4

Imperial	Metric
8 oz. cooked chicken	200 g. cooked chicken
4 oz. sliced lean ham	100 g. sliced lean ham
lettuce	lettuce
watercress or mustard and cress	watercress or mustard and cress
chicory	chicory
pickled onions	pickled onions
Cottage cheese sauce:	*Cottage cheese sauce:*
$1\frac{1}{2}$ level tablespoons redcurrant jelly ($1\frac{1}{2}$ oz.)	$1\frac{1}{2}$ level tablespoons redcurrant jelly (40 g.)
8 oz. cottage cheese	200 g. cottage cheese
1 level teaspoon horseradish cream	1 level teaspoon horseradish cream
$\frac{1}{4}$ pint thin cream	125 ml. thin cream
seasoning	seasoning

1. Arrange the sliced meat on a plate with the crisp lettuce leaves, cress, chicory and pickled onions.
2. To make the sauce, melt the redcurrant jelly over a low heat; cool slightly.
3. Blend the ingredients, except the cream and seasoning, together. Fold in the cream and season to taste. Serve the salad with the sauce.

Variations

Use all chicken. A cottage cheese dressing blends with many salads. The jelly may be omitted and a little lemon juice and grated rind used in its place. If cottage cheese is unobtainable use finely grated Cheddar cheese instead.

Plantation ham rolls

Preparation time: 10 minutes
Main utensil: foil
Serves: 4

Imperial

Filling:

1 packet vegetable soup powder
1 carton soured cream (see note)
2 rings pineapple
4 oz. sweet corn
4 large slices ham (approximately 8 oz.)

Metric

Filling:

1 packet vegetable soup powder
1 carton soured cream (see note)
2 rings pineapple
100 g. sweet corn
4 large slices ham (approximately 200 g.)

1. Mix the vegetable soup powder with the soured cream.
2. Add the pineapple, chopped finely, and the well-drained sweet corn.
3. Chill thoroughly.
4. Divide the filling equally between the slices of ham, roll up, wrap in foil and chill until required.
5. When ready to serve, trim the ham rolls at each end and serve with salad.

Note: If you cannot get soured cream, use ¼ pint (142 ml.) whipped cream and 1 tablespoon lemon juice.

Dehydrated soup powder is not only useful for making a soup but it can be used for a stuffing as in this particular recipe.

Variations

Mushroom soup is extremely good in this recipe particularly when blended with 4–6 oz. (100–150 g.) cottage or cream cheese in place of the soured cream.

Glazed ham rolls: Use the above recipe and brush with half set aspic jelly. Allow to set then garnish with gherkin, tomato, etc.

Cold boiled beef and coleslaw

Preparation time: 15 minutes
Main utensils: sharp knife
Serves: 4

Imperial	Metric
1 lb. cold sliced beef	$\frac{1}{2}$ kg. cold sliced beef
Coleslaw:	*Coleslaw:*
$\frac{1}{2}$ small white cabbage (see note)	$\frac{1}{2}$ small white cabbage (see note)
1 diced apple	1 diced apple
few sticks celery	few sticks celery
few raisins	few raisins
French dressing (see page 17)	French dressing (see page 17)
2–3 tablespoons mayonnaise (see page 89)	2–3 tablespoons mayonnaise (see page 89)

1. Slice the beef neatly and arrange on a dish.
2. Shred the cabbage very finely.
3. Mix with the peeled, diced apple, chopped celery and the raisins. Mix the French dressing with the mayonnaise. Spoon this over the salad and toss well.

Note: If white cabbage is unobtainable then use the inside of any cabbage. Do not use coarse outer leaves. Sprouts can also be shredded and used.

Variations

Use cold roasted beef, boiled brisket or silverside of beef, salted if wished.

Add a little grated horseradish to dressing.

Danish salad

Preparation time: 15 minutes
Main utensil: mixing bowl
Serves: 3–4

Imperial	**Metric**
10 oz. canned or cooked asparagus	250 g. canned or cooked asparagus
3 oz. shrimps	75 g. shrimps
can mushrooms or 4 oz. raw mushrooms	can mushrooms or 100 g. raw mushrooms
lettuce or parsley	lettuce or parsley
Dressing:	*Dressing:*
½ clove garlic (crushed)	½ clove garlic (crushed)
good pinch salt	good pinch salt
shake pepper	shake pepper
½ teaspoon mustard	½ teaspoon mustard
1 tablespoon oil	1 tablespoon oil
2 tablespoons white vinegar	2 tablespoons white vinegar

1. Cut the well drained asparagus into neat pieces.
2. Put into a bowl and add the shrimps.
3. Drain the canned mushrooms well or wash and dry fresh mushrooms – they can be sliced unless very small.
4. Add to shrimps and mix thoroughly with the dressing.
5. To make the dressing, blend the garlic seasonings with the oil and vinegar (no sweetening need be added to this dressing).
6. Serve on a bed of lettuce topped with chopped parsley. This is excellent for a light meal or hors d'oeuvre.

Variations

Toss in mayonnaise rather than the salad dressing and flavour with a typical Scandinavian herb, chopped dill, instead of parsley. Use diced cheese and shrimps.

Marinated kipper salad

Cooking time: 20–30 minutes
Preparation time: 20 minutes
Main cooking utensil: saucepan
Serves: 4–6

Imperial	Metric
8–10 oz. cooked, cold potatoes, old or new	200–250 g. cooked, cold potatoes, old or new
4 tablespoons mayonnaise	4 tablespoons mayonnaise
1 dessert apple	1 dessert apple
2 sticks celery	2 sticks celery
paprika pepper	paprika pepper
2 large kippers or 4 kipper fillets	2 large kippers or 4 kipper fillets
can sweetcorn	can sweetcorn
French dressing (see page 17)	French dressing (see page 17)
To garnish:	*To garnish:*
lemon	lemon

1. Dice the cooked potatoes and mix with the mayonnaise, then add the chopped peeled apple and celery and pile in the centre of the dish. Sprinkle with paprika.
2. Remove the bones from whole kippers.
3. Cut the raw kippers into very narrow strips.
4. Put into a basin and mix with the well drained sweetcorn and French dressing, made as directed on page 17.
5. Arrange the kipper mixture round the potato salad.
6. Garnish with lemon slices or wedges.
7. Serve as cold as possible with brown bread and butter.

Variation

Mock smoked salmon – raw kipper marinated in French dressing for several hours – may be served instead of smoked salmon as an hors d'oeuvre.

Cauliflower plus

Cooked cauliflower with various sauces and stuffings is an excellent and quickly made dish.

Cauliflower cheese

Cook the cauliflower whole. Meanwhile make a cheese sauce with 1 oz. (25 g.) butter or margarine, 1 oz. (25 g.) flour, ½ pint (250 ml.) milk or use half milk and half cauliflower water. Bring the sauce to the boil and when it thickens season well; add 1 teaspoon made mustard. Add 3–6 oz. (75–150 g.) grated cheese at the last minute. Choose Cheddar, half Cheddar and half Parmesan, or add crumbled Danish blue cheese to make a change. Pour over the cauliflower. Brown under a hot grill for a few minutes, serve at once. Serves 3–4.

Cauliflower and egg savoury

Cook the cauliflower whole. Remove the centre part and chop the cauliflower. Make ½ pint (250 ml.) cheese sauce, as above, or a white sauce; keep hot. Heat 2 oz. (50 g.) butter in a pan, stir in 3 tablespoons thin cream, the chopped cauliflower centre and 4 eggs. Season well and scramble lightly. Spoon into the cauliflower 'case', top with the sauce and serve. Serves 4–5.

Cauliflower and salmon pie

Divide a cauliflower into neat sprigs. Cook in boiling salted water until just tender. Meanwhile make up ½ pint (250 ml.) white sauce, using 1 oz. (25 g.) butter or margarine, 1 oz. (25 g.) flour ½ pint (250 ml.) milk. Open a medium-sized can of salmon (use the cheaper pink salmon) flake the fish, blend with the sauce. Add any liquid from the can also. Strain the cauliflower, and arrange the sprigs in a hot dish. Top with the salmon mixture, then a layer of breadcrumbs. Brown in the oven or under the grill. Serves 4–5. Instead of salmon use tuna, cooked white fish, chopped cooked chicken, ham or canned luncheon meat.

Stuffed peppers

Cooking time: 20 minutes
Preparation time: 15 minutes
Main cooking utensils: 2 saucepans, steamer if wished
Serves: 4

Imperial	**Metric**
2 large green peppers	2 large green peppers
seasoning	seasoning
Cheese sauce:	*Cheese sauce:*
1 oz. butter	25 g. butter
1 oz. flour	25 g. flour
½ pint milk	125 ml. milk
seasoning	seasoning
4 oz. grated cheese	100 g. grated cheese
3 oz. well-drained cooked macaroni	75 g. well-drained cooked macaroni
To garnish:	*To garnish:*
watercress	watercress
bacon rolls	bacon rolls

1. Halve the peppers and remove the core and seeds.
2. Cook the peppers in boiling salted water until almost tender, or season and steam.
3. Drain well.
4. Make the sauce. Heat the butter and stir in the flour. Cook for 2–3 minutes. Remove from the heat and stir in the milk. Return to the heat, bring to the boil and cook until thickened, stirring all the time. Season, add the cheese and blend well.
5. Mix in the cooked, drained macaroni.
6. Fill the drained peppers with the cheese sauce and put in a heatproof dish. Brown under the grill for a few minutes and serve at once, garnished with watercress and bacon rolls.

Variation

Cheese stuffing may also be used in aubergines or marrow rings. These vegetables can be cooked as the pepper but remove centre pulp from aubergine, chop and add to sauce.

Tomatoes au gratin

Cooking time: 5 minutes under grill, or 15 minutes in oven
Preparation time: 10 minutes
Main cooking utensil: grill pan or ovenproof dish
Oven temperature: moderate (375°F., 190°C., Gas Mark 5)
Oven position: above centre
Serves: 4

Imperial
8 large firm tomatoes
seasoning
6 oz. Cheddar cheese, grated
Topping:
2 oz. Cheddar cheese, grated
fresh breadcrumbs
chopped parsley

Metric
8 large firm tomatoes
seasoning
150 g. Cheddar cheese, grated
Topping:
50 g. Cheddar cheese, grated
fresh breadcrumbs
chopped parsley

1. Cut the tops off the tomatoes.
2. Scoop out the pulp, chop this and mix with the seasoning and grated cheese. Pile back into the tomato cases.
3. Top with more grated cheese and fresh crumbs.
4. Put either under the grill until the cheese melts or in the oven for 15 minutes. Sprinkle with chopped parsley and serve with salad or on buttered toast.

Variations
Use chopped shrimps or hard-boiled egg instead of the cheese.

Stuffed tomatoes

Cooking time: 20 minutes
Preparation time: 20 minutes
Main cooking utensils: frying pan, ovenproof dish
Oven temperature: moderate (375°F., 190°C., Gas Mark 5)
Oven position: above centre
Serves: 3–6 (see note)

Imperial	**Metric**
6 large tomatoes	6 large tomatoes
1 oz. butter	25 g. butter
1–2 oz. mushrooms	25–50 g. mushrooms
1 small onion	1 small onion
3 oz. bacon	75 g. bacon
1–2 oz. grated cheese	25–50 g. grated cheese
2 oz. bread (without crusts)	50 g. bread (without crusts)
seasoning	seasoning
To garnish:	*To garnish:*
6 rounds bread	6 rounds bread
little fat	little fat

1. Wipe tomatoes, cut a slice from the rounded end (not the stalk end – they stand better this way).
2. Scoop out centres with a teaspoon and sieve or chop.
3. Heat butter and fry finely chopped mushrooms, onion and bacon for a few minutes.
4. Add cheese, the bread made into crumbs, seasoning and tomato pulp.
5. Pile into tomato cases, put into dish and bake for 10 minutes.
6. Add tomato 'lids' and cook for a further 5 minutes.
7. Meanwhile fry the bread in the fat until crisp and golden brown.
8. Lift tomatoes on to the fried bread and serve.

Note: This recipe serves 3 as a main dish or 6 as an hors d'oeuvre or vegetable.

Variations

Use extra cheese and more onion and omit the bacon.

Egg stuffed tomatoes: Choose very big tomatoes, remove the pulp (use in another dish). Break an egg into each tomato case. Bake until set.

Haddock omelette

Cooking time: few minutes plus time for cooking haddock
Preparation time: few minutes
Main cooking utensils: saucepan, omelette pan
Serves: 2

Imperial	**Metric**
4 oz. smoked haddock	100 g. smoked haddock
Filling:	*Filling:*
few cooked peas	few cooked peas
little butter	little butter
Omelette:	*Omelette:*
3–4 eggs	3–4 eggs
seasoning	seasoning
1 tablespoon water	1 tablespoon water
1 oz. butter	25 g. butter
To garnish:	*To garnish:*
sprig of parsley	sprig of parsley

1. Poach the haddock in a little water or milk until tender.
2. Strain, flake and heat with the peas and the butter while making the omelette.
3. Beat the eggs lightly. For this type of plain omelette the eggs should not be over-beaten. Season, add the water.
4. Heat the butter in the omelette pan.
5. Pour in the eggs and leave for a few seconds until the bottom of the egg sets lightly. Tip the pan and loosen the edges of the omelette so the liquid egg flows under all the time. Continue like this, 'working' the omelette, until set.
6. Put in the filling. Fold the omelette away from the handle, tip on to a hot plate or dish, and add the garnish.

Variations

Many fillings may be used instead, for instance, other fish, grated cheese, cooked vegetables.

Plain omelette

Cooking time: 3–4 minutes
Preparation time: few minutes depending on filling
Main cooking utensil: omelette pan
Serves: 2

Imperial

3–4 eggs
seasoning
1–2 tablespoons water (optional)
1 oz. butter or 1 tablespoon corn oil

Fillings:

grated cheese (add to beaten eggs)
OR
chopped fresh or dried herbs (add to beaten eggs)
OR
cooked mushrooms (add to beaten eggs or to cooked omelette before folding)
OR
cooked vegetables (as illustrated) or fish or meat add to omelette before folding)

Metric

3–4 eggs
seasoning
1–2 tablespoons water (optional)
25 g. butter or 1 tablespoon corn oil

Fillings:

grated cheese (add to beaten eggs)
OR
chopped fresh or dried herbs (add to beaten eggs)
OR
cooked mushrooms (add to beaten eggs or to cooked omelette before folding)
OR
cooked vegetables (as illustrated) or fish or meat (add to omelette before folding)

1. Beat eggs lightly with a fork. There is no need to beat hard with this type of omelette.
2. Add seasoning and water if wished.
3. Heat the butter, pour in the mixture.
4. Leave for about ½ minute to set on the bottom, then 'work'. To do this, tilt the pan and move the liquid on the top so that it flows to the edges of the pan, and under the cooked part of the egg.
5. Add the filling and fold. Serve at once.

Note: Important things about an omelette are: (a) A good pan. Try to keep one pan for omelettes and perhaps pancakes wiping rather than washing after use. (b) Quick cooking so that the eggs do not become tough. (c) Serving it as soon as possible.

Variations

Use any of the fillings above.

Omelette aux fines herbes: Add a pinch of chopped fresh or dried herbs to the egg before cooking.

To season new omelette pan

Heat gently with a little salt, rub this in with soft tissue paper. Heat butter or oil in the pan. Rub into the metal. Store.

Oven-baked omelette

Cooking time: 10–15 minutes
Preparation time: 10 minutes
Main cooking utensil: large shallow ovenproof dish
Oven temperature: hot (425–450°F., 220–230°C., Gas Mark 7–8)
Oven position: centre
Serves: 4

Imperial	**Metric**
1 oz. butter	25 g. butter
6 eggs	6 eggs
2 oz. cheese	50 g. cheese
2 skinned tomatoes	2 skinned tomatoes
1 teaspoon chopped parsley or chives	1 teaspoon chopped parsley or chives
seasoning	seasoning

1. Heat the butter for a few minutes.
2. Beat the eggs, then add the grated cheese, thinly sliced tomatoes, parsley and seasoning.
3. Pour into a dish.
4. Cook for 10–15 minutes in the oven until the egg mixture sets.
5. Serve at once, with a salad or potato crisps.

Note: Although this omelette is baked in the oven, care must be taken, as with every other omelette, that it is not over-cooked.

Variations

Add chopped green pepper, removing seeds and core. This may be blanched in boiling salted water for a few minutes before adding to the eggs.

Add chopped ham or shellfish in place of cheese.

Scrambled eggs à la reine

Cooking time: 10 minutes
Preparation time: 10 minutes
Main cooking utensils: 2 saucepans
Serves: 4

Imperial
2 oz. butter or margarine
6 oz. diced cooked chicken
2–3 oz. diced salami or ham
2 tablespoons tomato purée
pinch cayenne pepper
4 tablespoons chicken stock
1 clove garlic (optional)
6–8 eggs
seasoning
2 tablespoons milk or thin cream

Metric
50 g. butter or margarine
150 g. diced cooked chicken
50–75 g. diced salami or ham
2 tablespoons tomato purée
pinch cayenne pepper
4 tablespoons chicken stock
1 clove garlic (optional)
6–8 eggs
seasoning
2 tablespoons milk or thin cream

1. Heat the butter or margarine in one saucepan.
2. Add the chicken and salami or ham and warm gently. Do not overcook.
3. Put the tomato purée, pepper and stock into the second pan and heat.
4. Add the crushed clove of garlic, or, if a more delicate flavour is required, add the peeled whole clove and remove before serving.
5. Beat the eggs, seasoning and milk or cream.
6. Add to the chicken mixture and scramble lightly, by stirring gently over a low heat until the eggs are just set.
7. Spoon on to four plates and top with the tomato purée mixture. Serve with hot toast or rolls and butter.

Variation
Add flaked cooked or chopped shellfish and a little chopped fennel, dill or parsley instead of chicken and salami.

Baked eggs en cocotte

Cooking time: 25 minutes
Preparation time: 10 minutes
Main cooking utensils: 4 small ovenproof dishes, baking tray or sheet
Oven temperature: moderate (375°F., 190°C., Gas Mark 5)
Oven position: centre
Serves: 4

Imperial	**Metric**
1 oz. lard	25 g. lard
4 oz. mushrooms	100 g. mushrooms
4 eggs	4 eggs
seasoning	seasoning

1. Divide the lard between the dishes placed on the baking tray.
2. Place in the oven for about 5 minutes to melt the lard.
3. Wash and slice mushrooms (there is no need to peel them if they are the button kind) and add to the melted lard.
4. Return to oven and cook for about 10 minutes.
5. Break 1 egg into each dish on top of the mushrooms. Season.
6. Return to the oven and cook for another 10 minutes until the eggs are set. Serve on small plates, with hot toast.

Variations

Use asparagus tips instead of mushrooms or add grated cheese and cream over top of eggs before baking. Tiny pieces of crisp bacon can also be added to the eggs.

Welsh rarebit

Cooking time: 10–12 minutes
Preparation time: 10 minutes
Main cooking utensils: saucepan, grill pan
Serves: 4–6

Imperial	**Metric**
Welsh rarebit:	*Welsh rarebit:*
1 oz. butter	25 g. butter
1 oz. flour	25 g. flour
$\frac{1}{4}$ pint milk	125 ml. milk
1 teaspoon made mustard	1 teaspoon made mustard
seasoning	seasoning
8 oz. cheese (see note)	200 g. cheese (see note)
1 tablespoon beer or ale or Worcestershire sauce	1 tablespoon beer or ale or Worcestershire sauce
4–6 large slices of toast	4–6 large slices of toast
butter for toast	butter for toast

1. Heat the butter in a saucepan, stir in flour and cook steadily for several minutes.
2. Gradually add the cold milk and bring to the boil. Cook until smooth and thick.
3. Add the mustard, seasoning, most of the cheese and the beer.
4. Heat steadily, without boiling too quickly, until the cheese has melted.
5. Spread over the hot buttered toast and sprinkle with the remainder of the cheese.
6. Brown under the hot grill.

Note: Use Dutch Gouda or Edam for a soft creamy rarebit; Cheddar or Cheshire for a creamy mild flavour; mix with a little Parmesan to give a real 'bite'. Welsh rarebit mixture can be stored in a sealed container in the refrigerator.

Variation

Salami rarebit: Put slices of salami on the toast, top with the rarebit mixture, garnish with bacon rolls, sliced fresh apple and parsley.

Aberdeen rarebit

Cooking time: 10–15 minutes
Preparation time: 10 minutes
Main cooking utensil: grill pan
Serves: 4

Imperial
4 large slices bread
$1\frac{1}{2}$–2 oz. margarine or butter
8 kipper fillets
4 tomatoes
seasoning
Rarebit mixture:
8 oz. Cheddar cheese, grated
1 oz. margarine or butter
good shake cayenne pepper
pinch salt
good pinch dry mustard
1 tablespoon beer or milk
1 teaspoon Worcestershire sauce (or to taste)

Metric
4 large slices bread
40–50 g. margarine or butter
8 kipper fillets
4 tomatoes
seasoning
Rarebit mixture:
200 g. Cheddar cheese, grated
25 g. margarine or butter
good pinch cayenne pepper
pinch salt
good pinch dry mustard
1 tablespoon beer or milk
1 teaspoon Worcestershire sauce (or to taste)

1. Toast the bread, spread with some of the margarine or butter and keep hot.
2. Brush the kipper fillets with the rest of the margarine or butter and cook under a hot grill until tender; do not overcook.
3. Put the kipper fillets on to the hot toast, top with the sliced and lightly seasoned tomatoes and then with the rarebit mixture.
4. To make the rarebit mixture, blend all the ingredients together in a basin and spread over the tomatoes with a palette knife.
5. Heat for a few minutes under the grill until the cheese mixture melts. Serve as hot as possible.

Note: If a piece of foil is put on to the grid of the grill at stage 2 the kippers will not make it smell. Rarebit mixture can be made up and stored in the refrigerator in sealed containers.

Variation
Poach the kipper fillets in boiling water instead of cooking under the grill.

Cheese dreams

Cooking time: 5 minutes
Preparation time: 10 minutes
Main cooking utensil: frying pan
Serves: 4

Imperial	**Metric**
8 slices bread	8 slices bread
approximately 1 oz. butter	approximately 25 g. butter
2 oz. grated or thinly sliced cheese	50 g. grated or thinly sliced cheese
To coat:	*To coat:*
1–2 eggs	1–2 eggs
2 tablespoons milk	2 tablespoons milk
seasoning	seasoning
butter or fat for frying	butter or fat for frying
To garnish:	*To garnish:*
tomato	tomato
parsley	parsley

1. Butter the bread and make into sandwiches with the cheese.
2. Cut into neat fingers, removing the crusts.
3. Beat the egg or eggs and milk on a plate. Season.
4. Dip the fingers in this. Do not leave them in too long as they must be firm to fry.
5. Fry in the hot butter or fat until crisp and golden brown. Serve hot, garnished with tomato and parsley.

Variations

Hot toasted sandwiches: Make sandwiches of bread and butter as above, then put under the hot grill to toast on either side and serve at once.

Croque monsieur: Make sandwiches of bread and butter, Gruyère cheese and ham. Do not coat as above, but fry until crisp and golden brown.

Bacon crisps

Cooking time: few minutes
Preparation time: few minutes
Main cooking utensil: frying pan
Serves: 4

Imperial	Metric
8 thick rashers bacon (see note)	8 thick rashers bacon (see note)
8 slices bread	8 slices bread
tomato ketchup	tomato ketchup
2 eggs, beaten	2 eggs, beaten
seasoning	seasoning
To garnish:	*To garnish:*
parsley	parsley
4 tomatoes	4 tomatoes
broad beans	broad beans

1. Fry the bacon rashers lightly.
2. Cut the crusts off the bread.
3. Spread each slice with a little tomato ketchup.
4. On four of the slices lay the lightly fried rashers.
5. Cover with the remaining slices of bread and dip each sandwich in beaten egg, making sure they are well coated. Fry in melted bacon fat until golden brown on both sides; season lightly before serving.
6. Cut each in half and garnish with parsley. Serve accompanied by fried tomatoes and broad beans, or a green salad.

Note: You can use rashers cut from gammon slipper, middle gammon, corner gammon, long back, short back, back and ribs, top back, prime collar, top streaky, prime streaky, thin streaky. The cheaper streaky bacon is admirable in this particular dish. Some grocers sell small bacon pieces which are ideal in dishes where the bacon has to be chopped. Crisply fried bacon is delicious sprinkled on top of a soup.

Variation
Put slices of cheese on the bread as well as the bacon.

Baked beans suprème

Cooking time: 15 minutes
Preparation time: 15 minutes
Main cooking utensils: oil stove, frying pan, can opener
Serves: 4

Imperial	**Metric**
4 oz. mushrooms	100 g. mushrooms
1 oz. butter	25 g. butter
8 lambs' kidneys	8 lambs' kidneys
1 level tablespoon flour	1 level tablespoon flour
$\frac{1}{4}$ pint stock or water	125 ml. stock or water
1 tablespoon sherry or white wine	1 tablespoon sherry or white wine
seasoning	seasoning
16-oz. can baked beans in tomato sauce	454 g. can baked beans in tomato sauce
1 tablespoon single cream or top of the milk	1 tablespoon single cream or top of the milk

1. Slice the mushrooms, fry in the hot butter, then push to one side of the pan or tip on to a plate.
2. Halve the kidneys, brown these in the butter.
3. Add the flour and blend well with any butter and kidney juice remaining in the pan.
4. Add stock, wine and seasoning.
5. Bring to the boil and cook gently for 5 minutes.
6. Return mushrooms to pan, or move further over the heat, add the beans and stir in the cream.
7. Heat gently, do not boil.
8. Serve on a warmed serving dish.

Note: This is an ideal picnic dish if you are equipped with an oil stove and frying pan. If this is to be eaten on a picnic it can be put into a preheated wide necked vacuum flask.

Variation

Use small sausages instead of kidneys, omit cream.

Baked beans flamenco

Cooking time: 25 minutes
Preparation time: 10–15 minutes
Main cooking utensils: frying pan, ovenproof dish
Oven temperature: moderate (375°F., 190°C., Gas Mark 5)
Oven position: centre
Serves: 4

Imperial	Metric
2–3 rashers streaky bacon	2–3 rashers streaky bacon
1 clove garlic	1 clove garlic
1 tablespoon tomato ketchup	1 tablespoon tomato ketchup
1 level tablespoon paprika pepper	1 level tablespoon paprika pepper
pinch marjoram	pinch marjoram
2 16-oz. cans baked beans with sausages	2 454-g. cans baked beans with sausages
4 eggs	4 eggs

1. Cut the bacon into strips, remove the rind and cook lightly with crushed garlic.
2. Add tomato ketchup, paprika and marjoram.
3. Arrange the baked beans in an ovenproof dish with the bacon mixture on top.
4. Make four hollows in the beans and break an egg into each.
5. Cover and bake for approximately 20 minutes or until the eggs are set.

Variations

Fry the bacon and garlic, add flavouring and the beans etc., and top with fried or poached eggs.

To fry eggs

Heat a little fat in a pan – it should be hot enough to set the egg white immediately it goes into the pan. Fry 2–3 minutes.

To poach eggs

Lower eggs into boiling salted water. Cook steadily for 3–4 minutes. Or, heat butter in the metal cups of an egg poacher. Put in the eggs. Cook for 4–5 minutes over boiling water.

Corned beef risotto

Cooking time: 20–25 minutes
Preparation time: 15 minutes
Main cooking utensils: saucepan, grill
Serves: 4 large or 8 small portions

Imperial	Metric
1 small green pepper	1 small green pepper
1 onion	1 onion
2 oz. mushrooms	50 g. mushrooms
1 tablespoon oil or 1 oz. butter	1 tablespoon oil or 25 g. butter
4 oz. long-grain rice	100 g. long-grain rice
½ pint stock or water with ½ chicken stock cube	250 ml. stock or water with ½ chicken stock cube
8 slices bread	8 slices bread
12-oz. can corned beef	340-g. can corned beef
3 oz. cheese, finely grated	75 g. cheese, finely grated
To garnish:	*To garnish:*
chopped parsley	chopped parsley

1. Chop the green pepper, discarding core and seeds.
2. Fry the pepper, chopped onion and mushrooms in the butter or oil.
3. Add the rice and the stock and cook until the rice is tender.
4. Toast one side of the bread slices.
5. Place a slice of corned beef on the uncooked side and put under the grill for a few minutes to heat the beef.
6. Stir most of the cheese into the rice mixture, place on the corned beef.
7. Sprinkle with the rest of the cheese and brown under the grill. Serve at once, topped with the chopped parsley.

Variation

Instead of cooking the rice with the stock and pepper, you can use a can of Spanish rice.

Corn and ham fricassée

Cooking time: 15 minutes
Preparation time: 15 minutes
Main cooking utensil: saucepan
Serves: 6

Imperial
1-lb. can ham
1 small can sweetcorn
1 small can pineapple tidbits
or cubes
4 oz. mushrooms
1 oz. butter
Sauce:
water
1 small can evaporated milk
2 oz. flour
1 oz. butter
seasoning
pinch mixed herbs
cayenne pepper
To garnish:
pieces of pineapple
chopped parsley

Metric
454-g. can ham
1 small can sweetcorn
1 small can pineapple tidbits
or cubes
100 g. mushrooms
25 g. butter
Sauce:
water
1 small can evaporated milk
50 g. flour
25 g. butter
seasoning
pinch mixed herbs
cayenne pepper
To garnish:
pieces of pineapple
chopped parsley

1. Dice the ham neatly, drain the sweetcorn and the pineapple.
2. Slice the mushrooms neatly and fry in the first ounce of butter.
3. Add enough water to the evaporated milk to make a total of $\frac{3}{4}$ pint (400 ml.).
4. Blend the flour with the evaporated milk, add to the mushrooms with the second ounce of butter and seasonings.
5. Cook until smooth and thickened.
6. Add most of the pineapple, the sweetcorn and ham to the sauce.
7. Heat well for a few minutes.
8. Arrange on a hot dish, topped with pieces of pineapple and chopped parsley.
9. Serve with crisp toast as a snack or with boiled rice and peas for a main meal.

Variation
Use a small can of mushrooms in place of fresh mushrooms. Heat these for a few minutes before making the sauce.

Stuffed loaf

Cooking time: 15 minutes
Preparation time: 15 minutes
Main cooking utensils: baking tray, 2 saucepans
Oven temperature: moderate (350–375°F., 180–190°C., Gas Mark 4–5)
Oven position: above centre
Serves: 4–6

Imperial	**Metric**
1 small sandwich loaf	1 small sandwich loaf
2 oz. margarine	50 g. margarine
1 oz. flour	25 g. flour
½ pint milk	250 ml. milk
seasoning	seasoning
2 eggs	2 eggs
4 oz. cooked ham, tongue or other meat	100 g. cooked ham, tongue or other meat
4 oz. Cheddar, Dutch or processed cheese	100 g. Cheddar, Dutch or processed cheese
little chopped parsley	little chopped parsley
1–2 tablespoons chopped chives	1–2 tablespoons chopped chives

1. Cut a thin slice from one long side of the loaf.
2. Scoop out most of the crumb, keep this to make bread-crumbs.
3. Spread the inside of the loaf with just under half the margarine, replace the slice to form a 'lid' and heat in a moderate oven.
4. Make a white sauce of the rest of the margarine, the flour and milk, season well.
5. Meanwhile hard-boil the eggs, shell and chop.
6. Dice the meat; heat in the sauce.
7. Dice the cheese, stir into the sauce with the eggs, parsley and chives.
8. Remove the loaf from the oven, take off the 'lid', spoon the sauce mixture into the hollow shape. Serve at once, cut into thick slices.

Variation

Use heated stewed steak as a filling.

Bapburger

Cooking time: 10 minutes
Preparation time: 15 minutes
Main cooking utensil: frying pan
Serves: 4

Imperial
Hamburger:
12 oz. freshly minced rump steak
1 minced or grated onion
seasoning
1 egg
pinch mixed herbs
For frying:
1 oz. fat
For burger:
large flat 8-inch bread round
lettuce

Metric
Hamburger:
300 g. freshly minced rump steak
1 minced or grated onion
seasoning
1 egg
pinch mixed herbs
For frying:
25 g. fat
For burger:
large flat 25-cm. bread round
lettuce

1. Mix the beef with the rest of the ingredients and form into a round cake. If moist you can flour the outside slightly, but if handled with damp fingers this should not be necessary.
2. Heat fat in the pan and fry one side then turn very carefully so it does not break and fry the second side.
3. Split the bread, there is no need to butter it as the meat mixture is very moist.
4. Put in the hamburger and cover with the rest of the bread, add lettuce.
5. Serve cut into four quarters, with spring or pickling onions or olives, and tomatoes.

Variation

The mixture may be made into four smaller rounds and cooked like this then put into smaller rolls. For a more economical mixture add a grated raw potato and omit the egg. For a firmer mixture omit the egg and potato and add a little oatmeal, about 1 oz. (25 g.), or fine breadcrumbs.

Hasty prawn curry

Cooking time: 20 minutes
Preparation time: 15 minutes
Main cooking utensils: 2 saucepans
Serves: 4–6

Imperial	Metric
1 large onion	1 large onion
1 oz. butter	25 g. butter
½ oz. flour	15 g. flour
1 level dessertspoon curry powder	1 level dessertspoon curry powder
1 tablespoon mango chutney	1 tablespoon mango chutney
¾ pint water	375 ml. water
1 dessert apple	1 dessert apple
4-oz. packet frozen prawns	113-g. packet frozen prawns
2 16-oz. cans curried beans with sultanas	2 454-g. cans curried beans with sultanas
4–6 oz. Patna rice	100–150 g. Patna rice
1 level teaspoon turmeric	1 level teaspoon turmeric
To garnish:	*To garnish:*
a few unshelled prawns (optional)	a few unshelled prawns (optional)

1. Chop the onion and fry in the butter until lightly browned.
2. Blend the flour, curry powder and chutney together with a little of the water, add to the onion and cook for 3 minutes, stirring all the time.
3. Add the rest of the water and peeled chopped apple and bring to the boil.
4. Leave to simmer gently for 10–15 minutes, adding the prawns and beans after 10 minutes.
5. Meanwhile cook the rice with the turmeric in boiling salted water for 15 minutes.
6. Drain the rice and arrange on a serving dish with the curry in the middle. Garnish with prawns.

Variations

Use hard-boiled eggs instead of prawns or a mixture of eggs and prawns or shrimps. Instead of shellfish, use white fish – skin this, cut the fish into neat pieces, then put into the curry sauce at stage 4 and cook for about 8 minutes until tender but unbroken.

Creamed scampi

Cooking time: 10–12 minutes
Preparation time: 10 minutes
Main cooking utensil: frying pan
Serves: 4

Imperial
2 oz. butter
8 oz. scampi, large size
seasoning
1 oz. flour
$\frac{1}{2}$ pint single cream or evaporated milk or top of the milk
lemon juice
To garnish:
chopped parsley or chives

Metric
50 g. butter
200 g. scampi, large size
seasoning
25 g. flour
250 ml. single cream or evaporated milk or top of the milk
lemon juice
To garnish:
chopped parsley or chives

1. Melt the butter in a frying pan or heat-resisting skillet.
2. Toss the scampi in seasoned flour and fry carefully for 4–5 minutes. Add more butter if necessary and keep shaking the pan. Take care not to overcook the scampi.
3. Pour in the cream, evaporated milk or top of the milk to make a smooth sauce. Cook, stirring all the time.
4. Season with salt and pepper and lemon juice.
5. Garnish with chopped parsley or chives.
6. Either serve in the dish in which it was cooked or turn out on to a hot dish. Hand rye bread or hot toast and lemon wedges.

Variation
Cut plaice or sole into small pieces and fry as the scampi.

Plaice fillets with asparagus

Cooking time: 15 minutes
Preparation time: 5–7 minutes
Main cooking utensil: shallow ovenproof dish with lid or foil
Oven temperature: moderate (375°F., 190°C., Gas Mark 5)
Oven position: above centre
Serves: 4

Imperial	**Metric**
4 plaice fillets	4 plaice fillets
1 packet frozen asparagus spears or canned asparagus tips	1 packet frozen asparagus spears or canned asparagus tips
juice of ½ lemon	juice of ½ lemon
seasoning	seasoning
White sauce:	*White sauce:*
1 oz. butter or margarine	25 g. butter or margarine
1 oz. flour	25 g. flour
½ pint milk	250 ml. milk
seasoning	seasoning
To garnish:	*To garnish:*
1–2 oz. blanched almonds	25–50 g. blanched almonds

1. Skin the plaice fillets and wrap each around several spears of cooked frozen or canned asparagus.
2. Arrange in a shallow baking dish, sprinkle with lemon juice and season.
3. Cover with a lid or foil and bake until the fish is opaque.
4. Meanwhile, make the sauce. Heat the butter or margarine.
5. Remove from heat, stir in flour and cook gently for 2–3 minutes.
6. Gradually add the milk, return to the heat, bring to the boil and cook until thickened, stirring well. Season.
7. Place fish on a hot serving dish. Garnish with toasted almonds, and spoon over the sauce. Serve with peas and potatoes.

Jamaican plaice

Cooking time: 15 minutes
Preparation time: 10 minutes
Main cooking utensils: ovenproof dish, saucepan
Oven temperature: moderate (375°F., 190°C., Gas Mark 5)
Oven position: above centre
Serves: 4

Imperial
2–3 oz. butter
4 large plaice fillets
seasoning
2 bananas, sliced
2 oz. blanched almonds
juice of 1 lemon

Metric
50–75 g. butter
4 large plaice fillets
seasoning
2 bananas, sliced
50 g. blanched almonds
juice of 1 lemon

1. Melt the butter carefully.
2. Use a little to grease the dish, arrange the fish in it, season lightly and brush with more butter.
3. Cover with a lid or foil.
4. Cook until the fish is tender and opaque.
5. Fry the sliced banana in the rest of the butter for 2–3 minutes.
6. Arrange the fish on a hot dish.
7. Top with the bananas and the almonds tossed in the remaining butter and lemon juice. Serve with salad or green peas.

Variation
Use sole or whiting.

Grilled plaice and orange butter

Cooking time: 7 minutes
Preparation time: few minutes
Main cooking utensil: grill
Serves: 4 small or 2 large portions

Imperial	Metric
4 good-sized plaice fillets	4 good-sized plaice fillets
2 oranges	2 oranges
1 oz. butter	25 g. butter
seasoning	seasoning

1. Wash and dry the fish well.
2. Grate the rind from one orange and squeeze out the juice.
3. Blend the rind with most of the butter and a little seasoning.
4. Rub the rest of the butter over the grid of the grill pan so that the fish does not stick.
5. Heat the grill, then put the fish under it and cook until tender. Add the orange juice to flavour it as it cooks.
6. Garnish with segments of the second orange and serve with a green vegetable or green salad.

Variations

Use lemon rind and juice. Cut down the butter slightly and put the fish on foil so that it keeps in its juices and flavour.

Seafood à la crème

Cooking time: 15–20 minutes
Preparation time: 15 minutes
Main cooking utensil: ovenproof dish
Oven temperature: moderately hot (375–400°F., 190–200°C., Gas Mark 5–6)
Oven position: just above centre
Serves: 4

Imperial	**Metric**
1½ lb. filleted whole small turbot or halibut	¾ kg. filleted whole small turbot or halibut
seasoning	seasoning
juice of ½ lemon	juice of ½ lemon
4–5 tablespoons thick cream	4–5 tablespoons thick cream
2 oz. grated Parmesan cheese	50 g. grated Parmesan cheese
1 oz. butter	25 g. butter
To garnish:	*To garnish:*
parsley	parsley

1. Remove the skin from the fish and place the fillets in a baking dish so that the fish looks whole again.
2. Season, add the lemon juice.
3. Pour over the cream.
4. Sprinkle with Parmesan cheese, dot with butter.
5. Bake in the oven. Spoon over the cream once or twice during cooking.
6. Garnish with a sprig of parsley. Serve hot with mixed vegetables.

Variation

Use cheaper white fish, e.g., whiting, codling.

Swiss herrings

Cooking time: 7–10 minutes
Preparation time: few minutes
Main cooking utensil: grill pan
Serves: 4

Imperial	**Metric**
4 herrings	4 herrings
seasoning	seasoning
about 3 teaspoons French mustard	about 3 teaspoons French mustard
4 portions processed Swiss Gruyère cheese	4 portions processed Swiss Gruyère cheese
To garnish:	*To garnish:*
parsley	parsley
lemon	lemon

1. Split open the herrings and remove backbone. Season.
2. Brush the flesh side with French mustard and place under the grill for 3 minutes, folding the herring again.
3. When nearly cooked arrange a portion of processed Gruyère cheese horizontally on each fillet and continue gently grilling until the cheese has melted and the fillets are cooked.
4. Garnish with parsley and lemon and serve at once.

Variation
A pinch of curry powder could be added to the French mustard and a few drops of Worcestershire sauce.

Kipper and lemon

Cooking time: few minutes
Preparation time: few minutes
Main utensil: dish or jug
Serves: 2

Imperial	Metric
2 kippers	2 kippers
boiling water	boiling water
To garnish:	*To garnish:*
slices of orange or lemon	slices of orange or lemon
parsley	parsley

1. Put the fish in a dish, then pour over the boiling water.
2. Leave for a few minutes until tender, lift out of the water.
3. Put under the grill if wished to crisp slightly, brushing first with a little melted butter.
4. Garnish with slices of orange and parsley or use lemon instead, and serve.

Note: Kippers make a good breakfast or supper dish.

Variation
Grill the kippers with a knob of butter.

Mackerel with fried crumbs

Cooking time: 15 minutes
Preparation time: 5–10 minutes
Main cooking utensil: frying pan
Serves: 4

Imperial
4 large mackerel
2–3 oz. fine breadcrumbs
2 oz. butter
seasoning
To garnish:
paprika pepper
parsley
lemon

Metric
4 large mackerel
50–75 g. fine breadcrumbs
50 g. butter
seasoning
To garnish:
paprika pepper
parsley
lemon

1. Remove the head from each mackerel, split the body and remove the backbones and intestines. Wash and dry the fish carefully.
2. Fry the crumbs in 1 oz. (25 g.) butter until crisp and golden brown. Put on a plate and keep warm.
3. Fry the seasoned mackerel steadily until tender.
4. Drain on absorbent kitchen or tissue paper.
5. Arrange on a dish, top with the crumbs and garnish with paprika pepper, sprigs of parsley and wedges of lemon. Serve with salad or mixed vegetables.

Note: Mackerel is a very highly perishable fish and should not be stored for any length of time, even in the refrigerator.

Variation
Use fresh herrings instead of mackerel.

Trout and mustard sauce

Cooking time: 12 minutes
Preparation time: 15 minutes
Main cooking utensil: frying pan
Serves: 4

Imperial
4 trout
½ oz. flour
seasoning
2–3 oz. butter
2–3 oz. blanched almonds
Sauce rémoulade:
¼ pint mayonnaise
½ teaspoon made mustard
2 teaspoons chopped herbs (parsley, chervil, tarragon, chives)
few capers

Metric
4 trout
15 g. flour
seasoning
50–75 g. butter
50–75 g. blanched almonds
Sauce rémoulade:
150 ml. mayonnaise
½ teaspoon made mustard
2 teaspoons chopped herbs (parsley, chervil, tarragon chives)
few capers

1. Remove the heads from the fish and clean out the intestines.
2. Wipe the fish and dry well. Coat lightly in seasoned flour.
3. Fry steadily for about 8 minutes in hot butter, then lift on to a hot dish.
4. Add the almonds to the butter remaining in the pan and fry for a few minutes. Spoon over the top of the fish.
5. To make the sauce, blend the mayonnaise with the mustard and chopped herbs and capers.
6. Serve the fish with the sauce in a sauceboat.

Variation

Omit the sauce and serve the trout and almonds with a little extra butter, allowed to darken to golden brown, with a little chopped parsley and capers added.

Other fish could be served instead of trout.

Mayonnaise

Blend 1 egg yolk with a pinch of salt, pepper, mustard and sugar. Add 1 tablespoon vinegar or lemon juice, then gradually blend in the oil, drop by drop, beating well with a wooden spoon to make a smooth sauce. 1 egg yolk takes ¼–½ pint (150–200 ml.) oil, but a less oily dressing can be made if preferred.

Cod kebabs Ankara

Cooking time: 6–8 minutes
Preparation time: 15–20 minutes
Main cooking utensils: skewers, grill pan, saucepan
Serves: 4

Imperial	Metric
$1\frac{1}{2}$ lb. thick cod fillet	$\frac{3}{4}$ kg. thick cod fillet
1 small green pepper	1 small green pepper
4 small onions	4 small onions
2 tomatoes	2 tomatoes
4 button mushrooms	4 button mushrooms
4 bay leaves	4 bay leaves
2 oz. melted butter	50 g. melted butter
salt	salt
paprika pepper	paprika pepper

1. Cut the cod into large cubes.
2. Blanch the green pepper and onions by pouring on boiling water and leaving for 5 minutes.
3. Drain; cut the pepper into cubes.
4. Quarter the tomatoes.
5. Thread the fish cubes, vegetables and bay leaves on to four long skewers and brush with melted butter.
6. Season with salt and paprika pepper and grill for 6–8 minutes, turning once and brush with more butter. Serve sprinkled with parsley, on a bed of rice.

Variation

Brochettes de scampi portuguese: Cook 1–$1\frac{1}{4}$ lb. (400–500 g.) well seasoned scampi on skewers as above (about 15 minutes). Meanwhile make a tomato sauce by frying 1 lb. (400 g.) skinned, chopped tomatoes with 1 chopped onion and 1 clove garlic in oil. When soft add $\frac{1}{4}$ pint (125 ml.) white wine and seasoning. Serve scampi with the sauce.

Grilled cutlets américaine

Cooking time: 10–15 minutes
Preparation time: 5–10 minutes
Main cooking utensil: grill pan
Serves: 2

Imperial
2 large cod cutlets
seasoning
1 lemon
1 oz. butter
2 large tomatoes
To garnish:
parsley
lemon wedges

Metric
2 large cod cutlets
seasoning
1 lemon
25 g. butter
2 large tomatoes
To garnish:
parsley
lemon wedges

1. Tie the cutlets, if the fishmonger has not already done so, into a neat round.
2. Season and sprinkle with some of the lemon juice from half the lemon (saving the other half for garnish).
3. Brush one side of the cutlets with melted butter and cook under a hot grill for 5 minutes.
4. Turn, season, sprinkle with lemon juice, brush with butter and cook until tender.
5. Add the halved, seasoned tomatoes towards the end of the cooking time, brushing these also with melted butter.
6. Arrange on a hot dish and garnish with parsley and lemon. Serve with creamed potatoes.

Variations
Use cutlets of fresh haddock, turbot or halibut.
Cutlets au gratin: Sprinkle the second side with grated cheese and breadcrumbs before grilling.

Grilled cod steaks with almonds and mushrooms

Cooking time: 15 minutes
Preparation time: 15 minutes
Main cooking utensils: frying pan, grill pan
Serves: 4

Imperial	**Metric**
3–4 oz. butter	75–100 g. butter
4 cod steaks (preferably from tail)	4 cod steaks (preferably from tail)
seasoning	seasoning
1 oz. grated Parmesan cheese	25 g. grated Parmesan cheese
4 oz. blanched almonds	100 g. blanched almonds
4 oz. small button mushrooms	100 g. small button mushrooms
To garnish:	*To garnish:*
2–3 small tomatoes	2–3 small tomatoes
sprigs parsley	sprigs parsley

1. Melt the butter in a frying pan.
2. Brush the cod steaks on one side with a little butter and season lightly.
3. Put on the grid of the grill pan and cook until golden brown, then turn.
4. Season the second side, brush with butter and sprinkle with the cheese.
5. Continue cooking until golden brown and tender.
6. Meanwhile fry the almonds and mushrooms in the remaining butter.
7. Place the fish in the hot serving dish, then add the nuts and mushrooms.
8. Garnish with wedges of tomato and sprigs of parsley. Serve with a green vegetable and new or creamed potatoes.

Variation

Use turbot or other white fish, or whole trout. Instead of grilling the fish fry it in the pan before adding the nuts and mushrooms.

Curry cutlets

Cooking time: 15 minutes
Preparation time: 15 minutes
Main cooking utensils: saucepan and grill pan
Serves: 4

Imperial	Metric
1 onion, chopped	1 onion, chopped
2 oz. mushrooms, sliced	50 g. mushrooms, sliced
2 green peppers, finely chopped	2 green peppers, finely chopped
2 oz. melted butter	50 g. melted butter
1 medium-sized can tomatoes	1 medium-sized can tomatoes
2 teaspoons curry powder	2 teaspoons curry powder
1 teaspoon sugar	1 teaspoon sugar
seasoning	seasoning
4 medium-sized cutlets cod or haddock	4 medium-sized cutlets cod or haddock
juice of ½ lemon	juice of ½ lemon

1. Fry the onion, mushrooms and peppers in half the butter for 5 minutes.
2. Add the tomatoes, curry powder, sugar and seasoning, simmer gently for 10 minutes.
3. Put the cutlets of fish on the greased grid of the grill pan, season, brush with melted butter and flavour with lemon juice.
4. Cook under a hot grill for about 3 minutes, turn, season the second side, brush with the rest of the butter, add a litttle more lemon juice and continue to cook until tender and golden brown.
5. Arrange the curried vegetable mixture in a serving dish and top with the fish. Serve with boiled rice and chutney.

Variation

Devilled cod: Use only 1 teaspoon curry powder and 1 teaspoon Worcestershire sauce, and a pinch of cayenne pepper.

Fried fish in chive butter

Cooking time: 5–10 minutes according to type of fish used
Preparation time: 5–8 minutes
Main cooking utensil: frying pan
Serves: 4

Imperial	**Metric**
1½ lb. white fish, either whole fillets of sole, plaice or whiting or portions of cod, fresh haddock, turbot or halibut	¾ kg. white fish, either whole fillets of sole, plaice or whiting or portions of cod, fresh haddock, turbot or halibut
1 level tablespoon flour	1 level tablespoon flour
seasoning	seasoning
2–3 oz. butter	50–75 g. butter
2 tablespoons chopped chives	2 tablespoons chopped chives
To garnish:	*To garnish:*
parsley	parsley
lemon	lemon

1. Wash and fry the fish, coat lightly in the seasoned flour.
2. Melt the butter and fry the fish until tender.
3. Lift on to a hot dish.
4. Add the chives to the remaining butter and heat thoroughly.
5. Pour over the fish.
6. Garnish with parsley and lemon. Serve with plain boiled potatoes tossed in chopped parsley.

Variation

Fish meunière: Allow the butter to brown and add chopped parsley in place of chopped chives – use a little more butter than in the recipe above.

Barbecued lamb kebabs

Cooking time: 10 minutes plus time to cook rice
Preparation time: few minutes
Main cooking utensils: skewers and grill or barbecue fire
Serves: 6

Imperial
approximately $1\frac{1}{2}$ lb. lamb, cut from the leg
1 large orange
1 large green pepper
1–2 oz. butter
5–6 tomatoes
8 oz. mushrooms
To garnish:
cooked rice
red pepper
green pepper
little butter

Metric
approximately $\frac{3}{4}$ kg. lamb, cut from the leg
1 large orange
1 large green pepper
25–50 g. butter
5–6 tomatoes
200 g. mushrooms
To garnish:
cooked rice
red pepper
green pepper
little butter

1. Dice very tender lamb – young lamb is excellent.
2. Put on skewers with rings of orange and rings of green pepper – remove the core and seeds.
3. Cook under the grill, turning all the time and brushing with butter.
4. Halved tomatoes and mushrooms can be cooked at the same time.
5. Serve with boiled rice, mixed with chopped raw red and green pepper, and moistened with a little melted butter.

Note: This dish is ideal for cooking out of doors on a barbecue.

Kidney and bacon pilaff

Cooking time: 25–30 minutes
Preparation time: 15 minutes
Main cooking utensil: saucepan
Serves: 4

Imperial	**Metric**
4–6 lambs' or pigs' kidneys	4–6 lambs' or pigs' kidneys
4 oz. streaky bacon	100 g. streaky bacon
1 large onion	1 large onion
1–2 oz. fat or butter	25–50 g. fat or butter
$\frac{1}{2}$ pint stock	250 ml. stock
seasoning	seasoning
1 level dessertspoon cornflour	1 level dessertspoon cornflour
2–3 tablespoons water	2–3 tablespoons water

1. Skin and core the kidneys, cut into small pieces; cut the bacon into small pieces, slice the onion.
2. Heat the fat in the pan and fry the kidneys, bacon and onion together until the onion is soft and golden brown.
3. Pour in the stock, simmer for approximately 15 minutes, seasoning well.
4. Blend the cornflour with the water, add to the kidney mixture and cook for several minutes, stirring all the time. Arrange in a border of cooked rice or on toast.

Variations

Use $\frac{1}{4}$ pint (125 ml.) stock and $\frac{1}{4}$ pint (125 ml.) tomato juice; add 2–4 oz. (50–100 g.) sliced mushrooms to the onion; blend the cornflour with port wine instead of water.

Pork chops and frankfurters

Cooking time: 20 minutes
Preparation time: 20 minutes
Main cooking utensils: grill pan, saucepan, frying pan
Serves: 4

Imperial
4 small pork chops (see note)
seasoning
2–3 oz. melted butter
4–8 frankfurters
1 green pepper (optional)
2 small eating apples
1 can sauerkraut (about 12 oz.)
To garnish:
parsley

Metric
4 small pork chops (see note)
seasoning
50–75 g. melted butter
4–8 frankfurters
1 green pepper (optional)
2 small eating apples
1 can sauerkraut (about 340 g.)
To garnish:
parsley

1. Season the pork chops. If they are very lean brush with a little melted butter. Grill until tender, turning over and lowering the heat when browned on either side.
2. Simmer the frankfurters in boiling water for 5 minutes, then drain.
3. Fry the cored sliced pepper and apples in the rest of the butter, add the sauerkraut and heat thoroughly.
4. Put the apple mixture on to a hot dish, top with the chops and frankfurters and garnish with parsley. Sliced raw tomatoes are a good accompaniment, or grilled mushrooms.

Note: Choose loin or spare rib chops.

Variation
Use canned corn instead of sauerkraut.

Grilled gammon and pineapple

Cooking time: 15 minutes
Preparation time: few minutes
Main cooking utensil: grill pan
Serves: 3

Imperial	**Metric**
3 gammon steaks (see note)	3 gammon steaks (see note)
1 oz. butter	25 g. butter
small can pineapple rings	small can pineapple rings
To garnish:	*To garnish:*
few glacé cherries	few glacé cherries
parsley	parsley

1. Remove the skin from the pieces of gammon.
2. Snip the fat at intervals – this prevents the rashers curling and helps the fat to crisp.
3. Put the gammon on the grid of the grill pan and brush the lean meat with melted butter.
4. It is important not to preheat the grill when cooking gammon or bacon, otherwise it curls before it is cooked, and the fat could burn. Grill quickly on each side, then lower the heat and cook through to the middle.
5. Just before serving add the rings of pineapple and heat thoroughly. Arrange on a hot dish, top the pineapple with glacé cherries and parsley.

Note: Gammon is a lean piece of bacon, so brush well with butter as it cooks.

Variation
Use peaches instead of pineapple.

Veal with Tyrol sauce

Cooking time: 10 minutes
Preparation time: 10 minutes
Main cooking utensils: frying pan, basin and saucepan or double saucepan
Serves: 4

Imperial

4 fillets veal

To coat:

½ oz. flour

seasoning

1 egg

crisp breadcrumbs

lard or butter for frying

Sauce:

¼ pint soured cream or fresh cream

1 tablespoon lemon juice

1 egg yolk

seasoning

½ teaspoon made mustard

2 tablespoons sliced olives

To garnish:

rolled anchovy fillets

Metric

4 fillets veal

To coat:

15 g. flour

seasoning

1 egg

crisp breadcrumbs

lard or butter for frying

Sauce:

125 ml. soured cream or fresh cream

1 tablespoon lemon juice

1 egg yolk

seasoning

½ teaspoon made mustard

2 tablespoons sliced olives

To garnish:

rolled anchovy fillets

1. Trim off any fat from the meat.
2. If the slices are too thick, flatten with a rolling pin.
3. Mix the flour and seasoning.
4. Coat the meat in this, then in beaten egg and crisp breadcrumbs.
5. Heat the fat.
6. Fry the meat until golden brown on the underside, turn and brown on the second side.
7. Then lower the heat and cook for several minutes to make certain the veal is tender.
8. Put all the ingredients for the sauce into the top of the double saucepan, or basin over hot water, and heat gently.
9. Pour sauce over fillets just before serving, and top with anchovy fillets.

Variation

Flavour sauce with a little paprika. Do not coat the veal but simply fry in butter until tender.

Escalopes of veal

Cooking time: 10 minutes
Preparation time: 5 minutes
Main cooking utensil: large frying pan
Serves: 4

Imperial	**Metric**
4 fillets veal (thin slices cut from the leg)	4 fillets veal (thin slices cut from the leg)
$\frac{1}{2}$ oz. flour	15 g. flour
seasoning	seasoning
1 egg	1 egg
crisp breadcrumbs	crisp breadcrumbs
pure fat or lard for frying	pure fat or lard for frying
To garnish:	*To garnish:*
rings of lemon	rings of lemon
1 chopped hard-boiled egg (optional)	1 chopped hard-boiled egg (optional)
chopped parsley	chopped parsley

1. Trim off any fat from the meat.
2. If the slices are too thick, flatten them with a rolling pin.
3. Mix the flour and seasoning.
4. Coat the meat in this, then in beaten egg and crisp breadcrumbs.
5. Heat the fat.
6. Fry the meat until golden brown on the underside, turn and brown on the second side.
7. Then lower the heat and cook for several minutes to make certain the veal is tender.
8. Drain the veal on absorbent paper and lift on to a hot dish. Garnish and serve with salad or a green vegetable.

Note: This meat may be lightly fried in a pan, then finished in the oven. This makes it an easier dish to serve when entertaining. Do not cover in the oven so that it remains crisp.

Variation

Add anchovy fillets to the egg, top with fried eggs or serve with pasta.

Veal cordon bleu

Cooking time: 15 minutes
Preparation time: 15 minutes
Main cooking utensil: frying pan
Serves: 4

Imperial
4 slices ham, half the size of the veal.
4 slices Gruyère cheese, the size of the ham
4 fillets veal
To coat:
½ oz. flour
seasoning
1 egg
crisp breadcrumbs
pure fat or lard for frying
To garnish:
rings of lemon

Metric
4 slices ham, half the size of the veal
4 slices Gruyère cheese, the size of the ham
4 fillets veal
To coat:
15 g. flour
seasoning
1 egg
crisp breadcrumbs
pure fat or lard for frying
To garnish:
rings of lemon

1. Sandwich the ham and cheese between the folded fillets of veal.
2. Mix the flour and seasoning.
3. Coat the meat in this, then in beaten egg and crisp breadcrumbs.
4. Heat the fat.
5. Fry the meat until golden brown on the underside, turn and brown on the second side – allow long enough for the heat to penetrate through to the ham and cheese.
6. Garnish with the lemon and serve with a green vegetable or salad, and creamed or new potatoes.

Note: Care must be taken in this particular dish that the veal is not fried too quickly on the outside, otherwise it will become hard and dry before the ham and cheese are hot. Never overcook this dish as the cheese becomes tough.

Variation
If preferred, the veal may be fried in butter, without coating, topped with the slices of ham, then cheese, and browned under the grill.

Grilled steak

Cooking time: see method
Preparation time: few minutes
Main cooking utensil: grill pan
Allow: 6–8 oz. per person

Cuts of beef to choose for grilling:
minute – very thin slice
rump – excellent flavour
fillet – very tender
sirloin – very tender
entrecôte – from ribs of sirloin
point – from pointed end of rump
porterhouse – large sirloin steak for 4
tournedos – fillet tied into rounds
To cook:
little butter or oil

1. Light or switch on the grill for several minutes before cooking the steak.
2. Put the steak on the grid of grill pan and brush with melted butter or oil.
3. Cook on one side, then turn with tongs – do not put the prongs of a fork into meat. Brush the second side with butter and cook to taste.
Minute steak: 1 minute cooking each side.
Under-done steak ('rare'): About ¾ inch (2 cm.) thick, 3–4 minutes each side.
Medium done: Cook as under-done, then lower heat for a further 3 minutes.
Well-done steak: Cook as under-done, then lower heat for further 5–6 minutes.
4. Serve with grilled tomatoes, chips, watercress and maître d'hôtel butter.

To grill tomatoes
Put into the grill pan with butter or margarine, cook for a few minutes under the grill before putting on the grid with the steak.

Parsley butter
Work chopped parsley and lemon juice into butter, chill before shaping. (Parsley butter is the English name for maître d'hôtel butter.)

Grilled chicken

Cooking time: 15–20 minutes
Preparation time: 5–8 minutes
Main cooking utensil: grill pan
Serves: 4

Imperial	**Metric**
4 joints of young chicken	4 joints of young chicken
1–2 oz. butter	25–50 g. butter
seasoning	seasoning
squeeze lemon juice (optional)	squeeze lemon juice (optional)
Additional accompaniments:	*Additional accompaniments:*
whole or sliced mushrooms	whole or sliced mushrooms
whole or halved tomatoes	whole or halved tomatoes
little butter	little butter
seasoning	seasoning
bacon rashers	bacon rashers

1. Put the chicken joints on to the grid of the grill pan if you can get this a reasonable distance away from the grill. If your grill compartment is very shallow, then it is better to put the chicken in the actual grill pan.
2. Brush with a little melted butter and season lightly; a squeeze of lemon juice adds flavour.
3. Heat the grill, put the chicken under.
4. Allow 4–5 minutes on either side with the grill at maximum heat.
5. Turn the heat lower and allow a further 8–12 minutes.
6. Grill sliced or whole mushrooms and/or tomatoes at the same time. Brush with melted butter and season. Add chopped or whole rashers of bacon during cooking. Serve with a green vegetable.

Grapefruit meringue

Cooking time: 10–15 minutes
Preparation time: 10 minutes
Main cooking utensil: baking sheet or tray
Oven temperature: very moderate (325–350°F., 170–180°C., Gas Mark 3–4)
Oven position: centre
Serves: 4

Imperial	Metric
2 grapefruit	2 grapefruit
4 teaspoons sugar	4 teaspoons sugar
Meringue:	*Meringue:*
2 egg whites	2 egg whites
2 oz. castor sugar	55 g. castor sugar

1. Halve the grapefruit.
2. With a sharp knife, cut around each grapefruit segment to loosen flesh.
3. Sprinkle each half with a teaspoon of sugar.
4. Whisk the egg whites very stiffly. Gradually beat in the castor sugar.
5. Pipe the meringue on to the grapefruit halves.
6. Bake until lightly browned. Serve alone or with cream.

Variation

To serve as a cold sweet, use twice the amount of sugar and bake for approximately 1 hour in a very cool oven (250–275°F., 130–140°C., Gas Mark $\frac{1}{2}$–1). Use really large oranges instead of grapefruit. Allow one per person and cut a slice off the top.

Orange and sultana syllabub

Preparation time: 10 minutes
Main utensils: 2 mixing bowls
Serves: 4

Imperial	**Metric**
3 egg whites	3 egg whites
2 oz. castor sugar	50 g. castor sugar
juice of ½ orange	juice of ½ orange
¼ pint sweet white wine	125 ml. sweet white wine
½ pint double cream	250 ml. double cream
small can mandarin oranges	small can mandarin oranges
4 oz. sultanas	100 g. sultanas

1. Whisk the egg whites until very stiff.
2. Gradually beat in the sugar until the mixture is very stiff.
3. Gradually fold in orange juice and wine; the egg will become softer, but still keep its fluffy texture.
4. Whisk the cream until just stiff – do not overwhip it – then fold it into the egg white mixture.
5. Drain oranges thoroughly and add to the syllabub with the sultanas. Serve in tall glasses.

Variation

Use a little less wine and add 2 tablespoons brandy; soak the sultanas in the brandy for a few hours.

To whip egg whites

Make sure the whisk is absolutely dry and clean, even a smear of grease prevents the egg white becoming stiff. Use eggs over 24 hours old, remove from refrigerator an hour before using; whisk in a large basin.

Pineapple Alaska

Cooking time: 2–3 minutes
Preparation time: 15 minutes
Main cooking utensils: 6 ovenproof serving plates, cloth piping bag with $\frac{1}{4}$-inch ($\frac{1}{2}$-cm.) plain pipe (optional)
Oven temperature: very hot (450–475°F., 230–240°C., Gas Mark 8–9)
Oven position: centre
Serves: 6

Imperial
1 raspberry-jam-filled Swiss roll
6 slices fresh or canned pineapple
1 block vanilla ice cream (to give 6 portions)
Meringue:
3 egg whites
3 oz. castor sugar
1 oz. currants
1–2 pieces angelica, about $1\frac{1}{2}$ inches in length (see note)

Metric
1 raspberry-jam-filled Swiss roll
6 slices fresh or canned pineapple
1 block vanilla ice cream (to give 6 portions)
Meringue:
3 egg whites
85 g. castor sugar
25 g. currants
1–2 pieces angelica, about 4 cm. in length (see note)

1. Cut the Swiss roll into 6 slices and put on to the serving plates.
2. Top each slice with a pineapple slice (drain canned pineapple well).
3. Put a portion of ice cream in the centre of the pineapple (make sure it is very firm and hard).
4. Cover with meringue as quickly as possible. To make the meringue whisk the egg whites until very stiff then gradually whisk in half the sugar and fold in the remainder.
5. Spoon or pipe over the ice cream and pineapple and pile high to look like a miniature pineapple.
6. Press a few currants into the meringue to look like the 'eyes' and top with strips of angelica.
7. Put into a hot to very hot oven for 2–3 minutes only, until tipped with golden brown. Serve at once.

Note: Soak the angelica in a little warm water; this makes it easier to cut into thin strips.

Variation
Soak the Swiss roll with a little sherry, brandy or Kirsch before topping with pineapple.

Yoghurt parfait

Preparation time: few minutes
Main utensil: basin
Serves: 6

Imperial	**Metric**
about 1 lb. mixed raw or canned fruit, pears, strawberries, peaches, etc.	about $\frac{1}{2}$ kg. mixed raw or canned fruit, pears, strawberries, peaches, etc.
$\frac{3}{4}$ pint plain yoghurt	450 ml. plain yoghurt
1–2 oz. sugar	25–50 g. sugar
To decorate:	*To decorate:*
fresh strawberries	fresh strawberries

1. Cut the fruit into neat pieces and put into a basin with the yoghurt.
2. Mix together gently but carefully so that the fruit does not become softened, but keeps its firm look.
3. Add the sugar then pile into glasses.
4. Top with the strawberries. Serve as cold as possible, yoghurt is always nicer if thoroughly chilled.

Variation

Use lightly whipped cream in place of yoghurt. To lighten the cream whip about $\frac{1}{4}$ pint (150 ml.) double cream until just thick – do not overwhip – then gradually beat in $\frac{1}{2}$ pint (300 ml.) thin cream or if not available whip in top of the milk. If using top of the milk you will need nearly $\frac{1}{2}$ pint double cream, but the milk makes it less solid and rich; or whip $\frac{1}{2}$ pint cream lightly and fold in 2–3 stiffly beaten egg whites, or whip the fruit into ice cream.

Peanut fudge sundae

Preparation time: 5 minutes
Main utensil: mixing bowl
Serves: 4

Imperial	Metric
4 portions vanilla ice cream	4 portions vanilla ice cream
4 oz. seedless raisins	100 g. seedless raisins
Peanut sauce:	*Peanut sauce:*
4 level tablespoons peanut butter	4 level tablespoons peanut butter
6 level tablespoons golden syrup	6 level tablespoons golden syrup
1 tablespoon water	1 tablespoon water

1. To make the sauce, put the peanut butter into a mixing bowl.
2. Gradually add the syrup and water, stir until well blended.
3. Put a spoonful of sauce into each sundae glass, then a layer of ice cream and raisins.
4. Add a further layer of sauce, top with ice cream and more raisins. Serve in tall glasses.

Variations
Use different flavoured ice cream.

Use honey instead of golden syrup. Serve sauce hot instead of cold.

When fresh strawberries or raspberries are in season, these make a delicious contrast in flavour. Arrange layers between the ice cream and raisins.

Acknowledgements

The following photographs are by courtesy of:

Colmans Mustards: page 32
Danish Food Centre: page 106
Electricity Council: pages 44, 54
Flour Advisory Bureau: page 52
Fruit Producers' Council: pages 16, 18, 50, 104, 124
Green Giant: page 20
Herring Industry Bureau: pages 30, 84
Isleworth Polytechnic: pages 12, 118
Libby McNeill and Libby Limited: pages 62, 64
Lyons Maid Limited: page 122
New Zealand Lamb Information Bureau: page 100
Plumrose Limited: page 28
RHM Foods Limited: page 38
Van den Berghs Limited: page 112
White Fish Authority: pages 40, 72, 76, 78, 80, 86, 92, 98